BROTHERS & SISTERS
Family Poems

By Eloise Greenfield
Illustrated by Jan Spivey Gilchrist

Amistad

An Imprint of HarperCollinsPublishers

To the brothers and sisters, with love from your great-aunt:
Joshua Benton, Parker Benton, Malcolm Little, Patria Little,
Evan Dozier, Camryn Black Morris, Andrew Gray, Dominique Best,
Kadeeja Best, Gabriella Best, and Olivia Best.
—E.G.

To Reverend Marrice Coverson, founder of the Open Book Project for
children, and Mr. Gregory Jackson, superintendent of Ford Heights, IL,
schools. For your love and care of the important young minds
you work for.
—J.S.G.

Amistad is an imprint of HarperCollins Publishers.

Brothers & Sisters: Family Poems
Text copyright © 2009 by Eloise Greenfield
Illustrations copyright © 2009 by Jan Spivey Gilchrist
Manufactured in China.

Library of Congress Cataloging-in-Publication Data is available.
ISBN 978-0-06-056284-7 (trade bdg.) — ISBN 978-0-06-056285-4 (lib. bdg.)

Designed by Stephanie Bart-Horvath
1 2 3 4 5 6 7 8 9 10
❖
First Edition

CONTENTS

Brothers and Sisters

Brothers and sisters
can be dear,
can be company,
can bring cheer,
can start arguments,
can make noise,
can cause tears,
can break toys,
can be few
or can be many,
make me wish
I didn't have any.
Helpful, funny, and good one day,
next day, they get in my way.
Still, I think no matter what,
I'd rather have them
than not.

Brothers

Wrestling

I push him and he turns around,
I tackle him, he hits the ground.
We wrestle. We're rough.
We tangle. We're tough.
We sweat and yell and tug and spin,
and then he lets me win.

New Brothers

We had to get used to each other.
Just because my mother
married his father, it didn't mean
we were a perfect pair.
I eyed him and he eyed me,
trying to find out
which one wanted to be
the most important, the smartest,
the funniest, the best.
It was a tie.
Now, we're okay
and pretty much into
this brother thing.

Teen Brother

We used to have fun, but now we don't.
He used to like me, but now he won't
say three words in a whole long day.
Moody. Mom says, "It's okay.
He'll grow right past it in a little while."
When I'm a teen, I'll bet that I'll
still love to talk and play and smile
and laugh as much as I always did.
But what do I know? I'm just a kid.

Mad at Mom

He's mad at Mom and so am I,
even though I don't know why.
She must have said he couldn't go
to a party or to a show.
Or maybe he can't go out to play,
for getting in trouble at school today.
Whatever it is, I'm going to be
mad at Mom as long as he.
What's that Mom is saying now?
My friend's at the door? Oh, wow!
Well, right now, I'm going out.
I'll come back and help
my brother pout.

Grandpa and Great-Uncle Paul

My grandpa is the quiet one,
his brother talks a lot.
Whenever the weather is ninety degrees,
Grandpa just says, "It's hot!"
But his brother says, "Oh boy, is it steaming!
The way that summer sun is beaming,
no living soul should step outside
unless he wants to be fried."
They must have been a funny pair
when they were very small,
one who talked all day and one
who never talked at all.

Changes

I used to want
to be just like him,
walk, talk, dress
like my brother, Jim.
But now that I'm bigger,
I can see
that he's my brother,
but I'm me,
and that's exactly who
I want to be.

My Little Brother

I'm bigger than he is,
but does he care?
I tell him what to do
and when and how
to do it,
but he just yells,
"No! I don't want to go!"
"Leave me alone!"
"Stop it!"
Maybe when I'm almost a man,
he'll understand what it means
to be a big brother.

Family Room

For two whole years,
Dad wouldn't talk
to his brother, and his brother
wouldn't talk to him.
But today, Uncle Leonard
came to visit, and they sat together,
talking, in the family room.
Mom and I watched them
from across the hall, and when
they hugged, I wasn't a bit
surprised. They couldn't stay mad
in a room with a name like that.

Sisters

Birthday Present

I wonder if she'll like it,
I made it by myself.
Will she really wear it,
or just put it on the shelf?
I cut out two big circles,
and I sewed them into one,
I glued on lots of ribbons
and then the hat was done.
I wonder if she'll wear it.
Well, maybe not outside.
I think we'll laugh about it.
At least, she'll know I tried.

Let's Make Up

Let's make up, don't be mad,
you're the best sister I've ever had.
Of course, you are my only one,
but no other sister could be so much fun.
Hurry up, now, we have to make amends,
say we're sorry and still be friends.
The years will pass, and it soon will be
off to college for you, then me.
Not much time before we separate,
come on, sister, it's getting late.
Let's make up, don't be mad,
'cause you're the best sister I've ever had.

Grandma and Her Sisters

They make me laugh,
the three of them,
when they get together
and talk about the fun they had
when they were girls, back
in the old days.
They talk fast, talk
at the same time, letting
their words tumble,
too tickled to finish
their sentences. Sisters,
laughing, laughing
about being girls together.

Aunt Me

I push the stroller slowly.
My sister and her husband
walk close behind me,
ready to catch the baby
if I stumble. I won't.
If I ever hurt him,
I would have tears
as big as lollipops.
Thank you, big sister,
for making me an aunt.

Twin

Some days I like it,
some days I don't.
Sometimes, when
they call me Candace,
I want to say,
"I'm Angie! Angie!"
Can't they see that my eyes
are larger?
So what if it's only a millionth
of an inch?
I can tell the difference.
Why can't they?

Mad at Dad

She's mad at Dad, and so am I,
and I know the reason why.
She wanted to watch TV tonight,
but Dad said, "No, that's not all right,
not when tomorrow's a day for school,
not even once will I break that rule."
And that is why I'm going to be
mad at Dad as long as she.
What's that Dad is saying now?
Do we want some cake? And how!
At least I do, but she won't come.
Well, I'll get mad again
when I eat the last crumb. *Yummmm!*

Favorite Things

She likes chess, and I like sports,
she likes jeans, and I like shorts,
but on two things we do agree,
both of us like her
and me.

At the Home Place

I stand at the place where Mom
grew up. There is land and more land,
but just one house. Everything
she told me about is here,
and so is she, the child with one
sister. I can see her, see them,
playing, hear the long echoes
in their laughter, hear them
singing loud to shatter
the loneliness.

Who Is This Girl?

Who is this girl
who says sweet words
and has the softest touch?
I don't know who she is,
but I love her
very much.

Brothers and Sisters

Don't Talk Mean

You can't talk mean to my little sister,
not when I'm standing near.
I said don't talk mean to my little sister,
did I make that clear?
If you don't know who you're talking to,
you'd better find out, 'cause I'm telling you
she's the greatest, cutest little girl
the world will ever see,
so, if anybody doesn't treat her right,
they're going to hear from ME!

Last Laugh

Let's play a trick on Marcus
when he comes through the door.
We'll jump out and make faces,
and we'll grab him and we'll roar.
Oh, what's that howl behind us?
It's a monster. Run! Don't stay!
Whew! It's only Marcus,
he came in the other way.

Zigzag

Family reunion,
picnic,
brother and sister,
the fabulous soccer two,
block, kick, zigzag
down the long field,
don't get tired,
dodge each enemy
foot,
go left, go right,
zigzag,
keep the ball,
hear the cheers,
see the hole at the
goal. Quick!
Kick, kick!
SCORE!

A Sister Coming Home

All summer long,
I've had no one to tease,
my sister spent the summer
with our Aunt Louise.

I've saved up all my teases,
don't know which to choose,
should I hide her bedspread
or put peanuts in her shoes?

I'm watching out the window,
oh, here she comes at last,
why am I not running
to her room to fix it fast?

I think I'm glad to see her,
what can a brother do?
I guess I'll wait to tease her—
but just a day or two.

Slow Talker

You don't have to help me talk,
I know what to say,
you don't have to give me words,
you just get in the way.

I talk slower than you do,
I like to taste each word,
take my time and say it,
make sure that it's heard.

Stop coming into my space,
stop coming 'cross the line,
you take care of your words,
and I'll take care of mine.

Three on a Plane

On the plane,
we sit three across,
happy in our sister-brotherhood.
We play word games,
guess at the cloud shapes
below. We eat,
draw funny pictures,
try to stay awake,
but can't. We drift off,
wake up again
to the sound
of our mother's voice,
calling us.

The Two of Us

When we grow up,
we're going to have
our own big company,
Carter and Carter, Inc.
Side by side we'll sit
at the head of the meeting table,
say yes to this and
no to that. Maybe we'll make
movies or cars or cities.
We don't know yet,
but whatever we do,
we know we're going to do it
together.